Minimalism & Mental Health

Tips and Tricks for Simplifying Your Life

Allyson Hodge

Copyright © 2019 Allyson Hodge

All rights reserved.

ISBN: 9781703932041

Table of Contents

Introduction 5

What Does Having Too Much Stuff Actually Do to Us? 9

What You Should Know About Minimalism 12

Time for Action! Some General Rules for Decluttering 15

How to Start with Minimalism for Mental Balance 25

The Decluttering Process for Mental Clarity 32

Wardrobe Decluttering: Wear What You Love 37

Create a Perfect Wardrobe You'll Adore 41

Minimalism and Food: Eat What Truly Nourishes You 46

How to Create a Simple, Minimalist Kitchen You'll Enjoy Cooking in 48

The Minimalistic Workout: Exercise in a Joyful Way . 52

How to Create a Minimalistic Schedule and Do More of What Makes You Happy 57

How to Be a Minimalist and Raise Happy Kids 60

Don't Be a Snail: How to Travel like a Minimalist 66

The Art of Less: Slowing Down and Simplifying 68

Introduction

Are you one of those people who feel they are fading and losing an endless battle with stuff? Do you feel that everything would be easier, you would be more energized, productive, and focused, if only you didn't have to struggle to keep things under control?

Each morning, instead of enjoying your morning routine and preparing for a new day, you are wasting half an hour in front of your closet wondering what to wear. There are so many clothes, yet you wear almost the same, dull outfit every day. You need a change. In the end, you pick the same comfy pieces you constantly wear. As this is repeated over and over again, it seems that all of the clothes hanging there are a pure waste of space and money—and time, if you take into account your wasted mornings.

When you need to pack for a trip, after that first spark of joy, you wish you didn't have to go. Merely thinking about the tons of stuff you need to pack and carry with you makes traveling seem not so fun anymore. You travel like a snail, carrying your house with you. When you finally arrive at the destination, you are not excited anymore, but completely exhausted instead.

What do you think of going outside with the kids or doing a fun activity with them, like a DIY project or outdoor play? If your reaction is "Ha! Not fun at all," it's probably because it requires special preparation. You first have to find everything you need amid the mountains of stuff, then pull it out (making an even bigger mess), and then carry it around. You are already tired just thinking about that "fun" time together. Instead of relaxation and fun, all you have is more and more stress. Add to the picture a constant rush to get everywhere on time—to work, school, soccer, ballet—you name it. Not fun for you, not fun for the kids. Too much of everything.

From time to time you feel a boost of energy—you will finally declutter your belongings, sort all of your possessions, finish all those unfinished projects. But then you look around and already feel overwhelmed. There is an overflowing laundry basket, junk drawers full of every kind of thing, toys and their separated parts all around the house, and so on. Wherever you look, you see more and more stuff piling up. You give up again, discouraged. Maybe you'll do it one day, when everything settles down, when you're better organized, and you have more time. But the absurd thing here is that you won't feel organized, neat, or peaceful until you really do that. "One day" will never come.

Because when it finally comes, it will also be "today," so you can't count on your future self. You'll still be as unorganized, chaotic, messy, and confused as today if you don't change something. You start thinking that something's wrong with you. You are simply not capable of being tidy, organized, or of keeping your home in acceptable condition. Your to-do list, if you even remember to make it, will always be a mess, half-filled, and you will forget to do half of the tasks anyway. To comfort yourself, you might go shopping. A pair of nice shoes you don't need may quiet these unpleasant emotions.

Does this sound familiar?

Having too much stuff is so common in the modern world that it's not considered a problem at all. Our homes are full of so many different things that we don't even need. We have tons of crap we don't use at all, don't love, don't even like, but we feel obligated to keep it. We are convinced that more and bigger is better. The focus is on the quantity, not quality. Our cluttered houses and lives have a big impact on us, but we are often not aware of it. We are taught by modern consumerist philosophy that shopping is the cure for all of our troubles. So we spend more and more money on material stuff, making our homes even fuller, not aware that it will take us even further from ourselves. Many of us have financial problems, but we keep buying stuff we don't actually need. Why would anyone behave so irrationally?

At the heart of this is one wrong belief. We subconsciously believe that having more stuff will make us happy. But the truth is that feeling is fleeting. What we will truly gain is a lack of money (even debt), more clutter, more stress, and more items to clean and organize instead of spending time on fun activities and with our loved ones.

What Does Having Too Much Stuff Actually Do to Us?

Besides wasting money and time, clutter impacts us in many ways:

- It makes it hard for us to travel or move. You're not able to just walk away anymore. You become attached and captured by material things.

- It makes us stressed. It raises your cortisol levels so you feel tired and exhausted—you have to spend more energy to keep your focus and finish tasks. That's how the clutter drains your energy. High cortisol is harmful to your health.

- It distracts us from what really matters.

- It makes our thoughts disorganized and chaotic. It's hard to keep focused when there's chaos around you.

- It supports procrastination.

- It makes us anxious and depressed.

- Having too much stuff makes you feel unsatisfied.

- It makes you and your family prone to health issues like asthma and allergies, due to the higher amounts of dust or mold.

We become slaves of consumerism and materialism who believe that happiness is in our belongings. We get further and further from the truth. We become captured by false needs in a never-ending cycle—we buy things to feel better, but we don't, so we buy more. Maybe it is time to search for a solution in the opposite direction.

I've also been there, done that. It seemed I was losing the battle with always overflowing piles of stuff. I was diagnosed with an anxiety disorder and experienced random panic attacks. The level of stress in my life was unbearable, higher than ever before. Then, one day, I decided it was enough. I was determined to regain control over my house and my life. So I started seeking ways to improve things—the household, daily routine, habits, my health, and myself as a person.

One of the concepts that offered possible solutions was minimalism. Oh no, I thought, not again. If they are going to tell me that I should live with one single pair of pants and one fork in an apartment with bare walls like a jail, they can stop now. But this time, it was different. It clicked with me and I decided to give it a try.

I started the house tour with an empty basket and picked up everything that bothered me—all the broken parts of stuff, all sorts of knick-knacks, random papers, broken toys. I continued with my kitchen counters and didn't stop for days until, one morning; I noticed our home was completely free of clutter, tidy, and breathable.

Today, 15 years later, my space is still uncluttered and I don't possess anything I don't use, don't need, or don't love. Not only did I master the skill of minimalism, everything in my life has changed for the better. I overcame my mental issues and dramatically improved my relationships, health, work, and my satisfaction with life. Besides that, through consulting, I have helped many people and families do the same in their homes and lives.

The concept is simple, yet the benefits are so many and so significant that everybody should know about it. Everybody deserves to live a simple, balanced life and enjoy the home that shelters them. That's why I decided to share my knowledge and experience in this field with you.

But unlike other books about minimalism, this one won't advise you to get rid of everything but your bed and a toothbrush. Here you will find a more realistic, more human approach for real people—a proven and also innovative way to practice minimalism.

What You Should Know About Minimalism

Minimalism is not only about our possessions. Its basic principles can be applied to almost any area—tasks, goals, consumption, schedules, fashion, design, and much more. So if you are a stay-at-home mom, a student, a businessman, an artist, whatever you do, minimalism can be your key to success. It's an inevitable part of success because both share the same mindset. It will help you focus on what really matters, instead of unimportant details.

Minimalism is not a lack of anything. It is an intentional focus on basics, fundamentals. And it can't be the same for everyone. Each one of us decides on our priorities. What you consider clutter (both physically or mentally), can be useful or even a priority for someone else.

Minimalism is about getting rid of everything that's not important so you can focus all your energy, time, money, and attention on what really matters.

This is why no one can say it will "not work" in all fields or for everyone. It's why I can promise you will never look at things the same way after reading this book.

Minimalism & Mental Health

There are many benefits to practicing this lifestyle. Some of them are obvious at first sight, while others need time to reveal themselves.

Twenty benefits of minimalism that have an impact on your mental balance:

1. Less work, easier clean-up
2. More time for what truly matters
3. Less stress
4. Better health
5. Less spending
6. More time for hobbies
7. You can do more of what you love
8. Freedom
9. Less materialism and obsession with money
10. Good for the environment
11. Clarity and peace of mind
12. More time and energy for self-growth
13. Purpose and more life meaning
14. More happiness, joy, and fulfillment
15. Better relationships
16. More experiences and new memories
17. Mastering the art of letting go, not being attached to the past
18. More productivity
19. Less fear, more confidence
20. Inner peace

When was the last time you had time to go outside, enjoy talking a walk in the fresh air, playing with kids or a dog? Do you have time to smell the roses or to watch a sunset? Or are you are constantly in a hurry, running from one task to another in the everyday hustle and bustle, with a bouncing mind that doesn't know how to be in the present for more than two seconds at a time?

We naturally tend to have more and more of everything, to be busy, to gain and accumulate. But we need to redirect the process in the opposite direction to discover what really matters underneath it all.

You can have it all through having less.

Time for Action!
Some General Rules for Decluttering

Decluttering is a pretty personal thing. You examine your belongings according to which of them serve you and which don't. Each one of us knows what works for us, so it's best to develop your own approach to decluttering.

However, there are some general rules to follow that will increase your chances of finishing this project successfully and, even more importantly, to keep things that way.

1. The one-year rule

For each item, ask yourself if you have used it in the past year or so and if you will use it in the next year. If the answer is yes, keep it. If not, toss it. This rule applies to almost all sorts of things. If you haven't worn a piece of clothing for a year or even more, you don't need it in your wardrobe, even if it's seasonal or for extreme weather. If you used that kitchen gadget only once and never again, it really doesn't need to have a place on your countertop and collect dust. You can't always strictly hold to this rule for keepsakes or books, for example. But it's pretty useful as a general rule.

2. A place for everything and everything in its place. This is an evergreen recipe for organized homes from the time of our grannies and it still works perfectly. If you don't have a proper, declared space for each (even the smallest) item, forget about keeping the house organized. Sooner or later, the piles will build up throughout your house again.

3. What's once discarded, has to go out

It often happens that we pack boxes full of stuff to donate or throw away. But then we don't finish the process and those boxes or bags stay in our cars or our hallways for days, weeks, or—forever. More often than not, people get annoyed by this and keep those things in the garage or somewhere out of sight where they sit until who knows when. Respect this rule and once you begin the process of decluttering, be persistent, and bring it to its end. Put those bags and boxes in your car and the next time you go anywhere, drop them off at the charity center or in the trash.

4. Discard duplicates

This might be the easiest one. Take an empty box or a basket and go on a tour throughout your house. Grab everything you know that you possess two of. Put all the duplicates in the donation box. Who the heck needs two sets of measuring cups?

5. Ditch guilt

The true reason why we all keep the crazy amount of stuff we don't need or like or didn't even buy is that we feel we are supposed to keep them. Why would you be obligated to keep something? The emotion behind this belief is guilt. We often feel guilty about throwing away something we got as a gift. We think that the person who gave it to us may expect to see the item when she comes to visit. Or we feel guilty for tossing something that we spent a lot on. It cost us money, time, and effort. We wanted that item. How can we just discard it now? We might feel guilty about our past selves. We also feel that we are doing something bad if we throw away things from the past, our keepsakes and mementos. Say goodbye to guilt, my dear!

There's nothing bad about deciding what you want and what you don't. You are absolutely free to create the lifestyle you want. Give yourself permission to let go of everything that doesn't serve you—as those material things leave, so will that bitter feeling of guilt. You don't owe it to anyone to keep anything.

Whoever gave you that ugly vase or that purple sweater that makes you look like a zombie probably won't even notice if you still have it or not. The people who love you don't expect you to save their presents just to make them happy. Appreciate their love and be thankful for their attention. But these emotions have little or nothing to do with physical stuff.

If you feel guilty about getting rid of something expensive, remember that you don't owe it to anyone, not even to your past self, to keep stuff. People change, our lives change, our priorities and values change. It's perfectly normal that you don't value things the same way as before. Thank the item for serving you and being a part of your life. Then let it go.

The same goes for items with sentimental value. Many of us feel that we will betray our dear memories if we toss the things that connect us to past times. But the truth is that those items are not the same as our memories. Keep valuable moments in your memory, not in boxes full of stuff.

Maybe you think about all those poor people in the world and feel guilty for tossing away perfectly usable items in good condition. What you can do is to donate or give away everything that is in good condition. And that's the end of any guilt. If you can somehow help people who need it, don't hesitate to take action. But keeping your home cluttered won't help anyone anyway.

6. Not other people's clutter, please

Do you have other people's trinkets that have been waiting for ages to be taken back to their owners? Or even worse, are you familiar with situations like this? Someone wants to get rid of something, but he feels guilty about throwing it away, so he asks you if you want it. You think it would be impolite to say no, so a bunch of crap comes into your house.

Another example: your sister never gets back into shape after having a baby, so her clothes don't fit anymore. She asks you if you would want them, so now you can't close the closet door. You actually wear one piece of that newly-arrived pile, but you feel you are not allowed to toss the rest.

A friend of yours asks if you want to accept the clothes and toys their kids have outgrown. Now your playroom and kids' closets are full of all sorts of toys and clothes in different sizes. And so on. Someone buys a wrong tone of makeup and it ends up in your bathroom. This is a recipe for making your house into storage for other people's crap. From now on, if you want a beautiful, minimalistic home, be heartless. Whatever is anyone else's clutter has to go. If you don't keep yours, why would you store someone else's? You can still be polite and tell the truth—that you don't allow clutter to enter your home—just in kinder words.

7. Baby steps, continuous progress

My experience has shown that changing things little by little is the recipe to stay on the path and achieve your goal in the end. Big leaps won't take you far. Some people think that it's best to do as much as they can while the first boost of enthusiasm lasts. But that way, you'll become overwhelmed soon and just give up. You'll start hating decluttering and the whole minimalism thing, although your home is not what you want and you live a messy life.

Constant progress in small steps is the only proven way to stay true in the long run. Although you feel inspired and want to turn the whole house inside out, stop yourself. Plan your actions and stick to the plan. You are not supposed to do more than the task for that day. You want to become a minimalist, remember? No "more and more"—even when it's about work. The point is in enjoying minimalism from the beginning, not to start hating it because you are overwhelmed from the first day.

8. By rooms or by categories?

You can choose one approach or the other, it's up to you. If you choose to declutter by categories, you need to sort all of your stuff into categories. For example clothes, shoes, cosmetics, papers, toys, kitchen items, electronics, keepsakes, hobby supplies, cleaning items, and so on. Tackle one category at a time. Take all the items from a category, place them on the floor, and then decide on each of them. Everything you want to keep, put back in its place.

If you decide to declutter room by room, tackle only one room a day or even over a few days, if you have a lot of work. Start from the easiest one, because you will see progress soon and that will keep you motivated. It's pretty simple. However, one thing to be aware of is to make sure you don't just move your clutter from one room to another, but you actually declutter.

9. A clutter-free zone

This one is more useful as a trick for beginning to declutter than a rule. Declare a clutter-free zone. That might be a large zone, like a whole room, or a tiny one, like your nightstand. The rule is simple: no clutter in this area! Declutter it, tidy it up, and make all surfaces flat with nothing on them. And then keep it that way. When you manage to maintain that order for about 30 days in a row, you can extend your clutter-free zone. It can include one more drawer, one more part of a room, or even the next room. Practice this, keep your no-clutter zone tidy and minimalistic, and expand the area whenever it's time for it. If you are persistent in your efforts, soon you will have the whole house decluttered, neat, and minimalistic.

10. Try a challenge

If you like challenges, this may be a simple and fun way to step into a minimalist lifestyle. There are numerous suggestions for minimalist challenges online. You can try out some of them that sound right to you. Or you can use our minimalistic challenge that we'll offer later in this book.

Whichever challenge you decide to try, the goal is the same—to begin your minimalistic journey. The point is not in getting rid of most of your stuff while remaining in the same mental state, and going shopping to replace the discarded items. The main goal of any challenge should be to get you in the right mental state and with the attitude that will help you to become a true minimalist and to begin thinking like one.

11. Stay mindful

One of the main benefits you will get from a minimalist lifestyle is more mindfulness. This means you will have enough time and space to be truly present, here and now, and aware of everything around you and inside you. Wouldn't it be great to begin while you're still preparing to become a minimalist? This is a perfect time for practicing. Try to be as present as possible while you're decluttering. Pay attention to all sensations, to your emotions, to the energy that flows. You can slow the work down to have enough time for this. Don't declutter in a hurry, just to finish the task. Try to enjoy the process. If it would help, you can play some nice, relaxing music or light scented candles. Open all windows to enjoy the fresh air. The decluttering process shouldn't be just one more project and a task on your to-do list. It's also a process of self-exploration and inner work, so be gentle to yourself and stay mindful during the whole process.

12. Have fun!

Minimalism is all about the most important stuff. And there are few more important things in life than having fun. Research has shown that people stay persistent in sports and recreation and maintain their routines only under one condition—if it's fun.

I could say the same for decluttering. Of all of the people I worked with (and there were many!) only those who were finding the process fun succeeded in decluttering their houses completely and switching to a minimalist lifestyle.

Therefore, my advice to you is: make decluttering fun! You can do it alone or with a friend or a family member. Follow your muse, sing, dance, try on clothes, drink your favorite drink, eat something delicious, take frequent breaks, do whatever you want to make it fun. Just be careful not to turn toy decluttering, for example, into an all-day tea party with dolls and teddy bears or playing under tents made from bedsheets.

How to Start with Minimalism for Mental Balance

You want to become a minimalist, to gain clarity, focus on what matters the most, and feel several benefits. Congratulations! That's a wise decision and it will be game-changer.

But where to start? What should you do to begin changing your lifestyle for minimalism?

You can't just wake up the next morning as a minimalist. That's why we are sharing some advice with you on how to get started.

Make yourself a cup of coffee or your favorite tea. Why is that important? Because you have some serious work to do here, but you can also enjoy your new journey.

Ask the big questions

The first step is to decide on some essential things. First of all, what do you want? What do you want to be, to do, or to have? What does your dream life look like? What do you want more of? More clarity, more peace of mind, more joy? Write all those things down.

What brings you stress? Write that down. What brings you clarity? Write that down, too. What do you want instead of chaos and clutter? Why do you want to make more space in your life? What do you need it for? Now you know what you would like to eliminate and what to have more of in your life.

What's most important to you? Write down as many things as you can remember (at least five) that matter to you the most. These are the activities, people, emotions, and things that make it worth waking up in the morning—your kids, your spouse, your mission, your career, art and creating, travel, anything that brings a smile to your face. Those are your "whys." Those are the answers for every time you ask yourself, "Why am I doing this crazy minimalism project? Why do I need to change my lifestyle?" It's wise to have them all written down to remind yourself whenever you need it.

Visualize your perfect life. Imagine how awesome it would be. Imagine yourself living it. Try to imagine your emotions. Feel it as if it were real. Be creative and add as many details to your vision as possible. Imagine your home as you want it to be. Visualize yourself and your loved ones enjoying it. Relax and stay in this daydream for as long as you are comfortable. Remember that feeling, and you'll be able to come back to it in your thoughts whenever you need a reminder.

Make some decisions

Prioritize. Decide what those things you won't compromise on are. Those are probably the same things you listed as most important, those that make your life worth living. Minimalism is all about focusing on what is most important and eliminating everything else. So you have to be clear about what those fundamentals are. For example, it might be your family, your marriage, career, or your best friends.

Decide to commit the most of your energy and time to those four fields. Then you can go further in prioritizing. What's most important to you in family life? What lifestyle do you want for your family? Which atmosphere do you want in your home? Is the health of your loved ones among your priorities? Is it crucial to have enough quality time together? And so on.

What's most important to you in your marriage? Is it love, faith, parenting, activities together? Write down top priorities for each of your important areas. Choose at least three things for each of them. Now you have a clear view on the basics around which your world revolves.

Decide to make changes and simplify your life. Once you know why you're doing it and what you will get in return, it's not hard to decide to do what needs to be done. This final and written decision is a pretty powerful cure against giving up on it halfway.

Decide to choose quality over quantity

You have probably realized before now that more and bigger is not always better. It's one of the fundamental principles of minimalism. Having a full closet doesn't mean that you have something nice to wear and can feel both pretty and comfortable. Having a thousand followers on a social network doesn't mean that you have any true friends. A life full of stuff doesn't mean you have had worthwhile experiences and doesn't guarantee that you won't feel lonely when you come home. It's always better to read one single page of a great book than 500 worthless pages. Always keep in mind the true meaning of "enough" and insist on quality over quantity. Hold on to this rule whenever you make decisions.

Decide to let go

Minimalism is also the art of letting go. It says you should stop holding onto things that keep you stuck. This is applicable to everything in our lives—our belongings, people who drain our energy, limiting beliefs, bad habits, and everything else. A wonderful side of minimalism is that it will gradually teach you the art of letting go. You'll start simple, like with the items in your physical space, and then go further to other things in your life. Once you learn how to get rid of things that don't serve you, you'll know how to do that with your thoughts, emotions, memories, ideas, and so on.

Decide it's time for an internal, mental decluttering, too

If you don't want to get rid of mental clutter, your physical minimalism won't be long-lasting. That's because our physical environment is closely connected to our mental state. Starting a minimalistic lifestyle is the right time to begin your soul searching and self-development journey. Clean and decluttered mental space will accelerate your success in all fields in so many ways. Without this step, you'll soon find yourself surrounded by an excess of everything.

Look at the current situation

Walk through your entire home and all of your possessions. Notice what you possess. Is there too much of one kind of thing? Which aspects do you need to work on the most? Maybe you have an overflowing wardrobe, but not any excess in the kitchen. Or you want to get rid of boxes full of keepsakes, but to keep all of your books.

Do you keep stuff "just in case" or for a rainy day? Are you saving too many things from the past? Or do you save something for a future self who will be thinner, braver, different? Don't judge; just notice the current situation and the areas of your home and life that need most of your attention.

Check what you use and love. What are the things that add value to your life? Which mug do you pick on Monday mornings? Which pair of pants make you feel pretty? Which blanket is the softest to wrap yourself in while watching a movie? If you had to move immediately, what would you take with you?

Get inspired

After reading this book, and even before you finish it, you will surely feel excited about beginning these changes. And it's awesome! But this first boost of excitement will leave you in a few days. That's when you need something to inspire and motivate you again to go on with the project.

Some of the great ways to make these reminders are by creating a vision board, using Pinterest, reading, or watching videos about the minimalistic lifestyle. It's super helpful to be surrounded by the right kind of influence. Use the current accessibility of information and stay motivated.

If you can, go on a trip. Travel will remind you of what's important in life, but also how much easier traveling is (as with life in general) when you have less to carry with you.

Make a savings account for emergencies to reduce stress. Fear of lack and not having enough in a serious situation makes us stressed and, as an answer to that, we start hoarding. Piles of stuff won't help you in an emergency situation, but a fund will. Once you know you are safe, you'll be relaxed enough to let go.

Time for action!

As we said, a minimalist home is the perfect place to start living a minimalist lifestyle. So it's time to start decluttering. This will be exactly what we discuss in the next few chapters.

The Decluttering Process for Mental Clarity

Once you have decided to work by rooms or by categories, it's time to begin.

Big items: Walk through your home and see which big items you have but are not using. They just sit there, taking up place and serving as a placeholder for clothes or other stuff. It could be a tall lamp you never turn on, a coffee table in the corner, big boxes, or even a bouncing ball you never use.

Get everything out: If you have chosen to declutter by categories, pick the first of them. Take all the stuff of that type together and put them on the floor or a table. It's eye-opening to realize that you actually have 329 markers, 36 candles, or 17 umbrellas. Who the heck needs so many markers? That many candles would be enough to supply a church! And 17 umbrellas would be fine if it starts to rain and never stop again. That's why it's good to see all of the same kinds of belongings in one place.

If you have decided to declutter room by room, then start with one corner, a shelf, a dresser, etc. Empty it out completely. Put all the stuff on a flat surface. From here on, the process is the same for both approaches.

Throw away damaged things: Toss everything that is broken, torn, doesn't work, or has missing parts. There's no point in keeping them. You know you'll never fix little trinkets you actually don't need. Pencils without erasers, for instance.

Get rid of duplicates: Nobody needs two sets of measuring cups unless you're a restaurant chef. Even in that case, one set would probably be enough. Discard everything you have more than one of. Of course, this does not apply to some things like clothes or beddings—it's more of a general rule.

Two questions to ask yourself for each item: Do I use it? Do I like it? These will give you all the answers you need.

If you use it regularly, or even occasionally, it's ok to keep it. This criteria is different for different kinds of things. For instance, you can say you use a shirt if you wear it. Maybe not every day, but often. If you haven't worn it for over a year, you don't use it. But for a Christmas decoration or your brise-soleil, ask yourself, do you use it once a year? If you feel any resistance when it comes to discarding things you don't use, ask yourself why. If it's because you spent a lot on it, think about how much value you are giving to the money you have spent by keeping these items as clutter. On the other hand, they might serve someone else who needs them instead.

If you feel guilty for any reason, go back to the place where we talked about how to combat this emotion. It's super simple: if you don't use it, you don't need it. Toss it and you won't even notice it's gone. If you are afraid of throwing something away because you think you might need it again, there's a good trick for that. Pack all those things in a box, label it, and put it somewhere out of sight. If you don't need anything from it in the next six months, just discard the box without opening it.

The second important question to answer: Do you like it?

Life is not long enough to be surrounded by things you don't completely love. In fact, looking at it from this aspect, you deserve to use only stuff you completely adore every single day.

Decide to keep only items that make you feel joy. Out of all of the mugs, keep your favorite one. You can't sip coffee from more than one mug at the same time, can you? Why would you use any perfume except your favorite? Why wear any other pair of jeans when that one pair makes you look (and feel) amazing?

Don't keep your favorite pieces for special occasions—being alive is a special occasion already. Don't compromise anymore. You are not supposed to use things you don't like. You don't have to share your living space with them. You deserve to have only what makes you joyful. Be free to let go of everything else.

It's as simple as possible. Do I use this? If yes, keep it. If not, toss it. Do I like this? Yes—keep it. No—throw it away.

Time for decisions

In general, there are only two options for every item—it either stays or it has to go. That means you need two boxes or to make two piles: one for things to keep and the other for the things you're getting rid of. Put the belongings you want to keep in their place. The second pile should be divided into donation and garbage. The donation box is here for all those things that are in good condition, but you don't need or don't like them. Someone else might be happy to have and use them. You can also pass things on to friends and family, but only if you know for sure that they would like to have them.

Trash bags are here for an obvious reason—to hold everything that can't serve anyone anymore. Everything worn out, stained, broken, torn, or useless gets put onto the garbage pile or in trash bags.

If you find it particularly hard to decide on some items, you may have one more box or pile—the maybe box. Put the things you are not sure about here, but be careful not to overuse this option. The decision is waiting for you at the end anyway.

Wardrobe Decluttering: Wear What You Love

Decluttering your wardrobe is all about deciding what you love to wear and how you want to look. It can be tricky though, because we often feel that getting rid of pieces in perfect condition means that we wasted the money we spent on them. But your money was already wasted when you purchased them, right? Keeping them in your closet won't bring your money back. The only thing you can gain from them now is more free space—if you toss them out.

1. Streamline your vision and your idea of what you want your style to look like

You can find inspiration on Pinterest or the old-fashioned way, in magazines. If you use Pinterest, create a board for your fashion inspiration and pin outfits you love from top to bottom. Feel the vibe of all those images together. That's the feeling you should have whenever you open the closet. Look for your fantasy style. Do you gravitate to bright colors or dark? What kind of fabrics inspire you? What accessories do you like? Your wardrobe should be a place of happiness, not overflowing storage.

2. Focus on what you want to keep

Pick your favorite pieces and hang them up if you have some extra space in your room or somewhere outside of the purging area. These should include the jeans you live in, the top you wore three times just last week, the dress that makes you feel like a queen. These are the things you absolutely love and would pack in your suitcase for the weekend. In other words, you wear them all the time. If you are not sure about an item, it can't qualify for this category because you don't love it. In total, there could be three or 33 pieces, it's up to you. Set them aside and go back to the rest of your wardrobe. From this step forward, everything else is negotiable.

3. Try everything on

This step might be time-consuming, but it really helps a lot in making decisions. If you haven't worn an item for six months or longer, you may not accurately remember how it looks on you. So don't be lazy; try the clothes on. By doing this you will notice if a piece is in good condition, if it needs alterations, or if it's worth repairing. Don't hold on to clothes with holes or stains—you'll never look good in them. Even our favorite pieces get old and worn-out.

Do you like the color of the item? Do you have other pieces to pair it with? Evaluate if the item is flattering, does it highlight sections you want to present, does it skim over those you want to hide? Does the cut, the size, and fit work for your body? Are you more into looser clothes or are you more into fitted clothes?

4. How do I feel wearing this item?

There are far too many options, fashion styles, and retailers everywhere to compromise and wear something you don't feel great in.

5. Would I buy this again?

This is a very insightful question. Imagine you are in the store right now. Would you buy it again? This answer tells you everything you need to know about the place of this item in your life.

6. Does the item reflect and convey the style you want for yourself?

Does it have the same vibe as your Pinterest board? Does it fit into your vision of who you want to be and in which direction you want to grow? Maybe you have great memories in that silver top, but does it support the image of yourself you are building in the present?

7. What should I replace?

Maybe you can't afford to throw away some pieces you don't truly love, but need them. Write a list of those things and replace them one by one when you can.

8. Where will your discarded items go?

You can donate them to a charity or pass them on to friends or family. If something is expensive and in perfect condition, you can try to sell it online. The basic thing here is that your discarded things must be out of the house. Don't let yourself keep them in boxes in your car or hidden somewhere in your home. Finish your wardrobe decluttering with style.

9. For all those things you decided to keep, set your future re-evaluation date.

It may happen that you don't wear some of these things either within the next six months. That means you really don't need them. There's also an old, well-known trick to help you keep track of which items you wear. Turn all of your hangers backward on the rod, and then each item that you wear, hang them back the right way. You will easily see which items you really use and which you don't.

Create a Perfect Wardrobe You'll Adore

You already know why you're going minimal. Creating a minimalist wardrobe means that you won't have to waste time and energy on deciding what to wear or what you can combine to look all put together. You will never again stand in front of a full closet and have "nothing to wear." Instead, you'll always have nice outfits you enjoy, albeit with a smaller wardrobe, since you now understand that a minimalist wardrobe is a small collection of loved and useful clothes.

Once you have purged your clothes and have gotten rid of everything that you don't love and that doesn't fit into the style you want to cultivate, it's time to build your new wardrobe.

You might already have all of the basics or might need to purchase some new pieces for your capsule wardrobe. A capsule wardrobe is the concept of having a limited number of pieces that you can combine in multiple ways to create many outfits.

Converting from an overflowing to a capsule wardrobe is a meaningful step towards practicing conscious living. But it can also be overwhelming. This is why we created this guide to help you through the process of creating your first capsule wardrobe.

1. Choose your style and create a unique look

Your style should represent who you are. You definitely need to add some personality to this kind of self-expression. Consider what works for you. Something that is a must-have for others might be useless to you. For instance, you can't use a little black dress if you don't go out and spend all of your spare time with kids on a playground. Pencil skirts and high bottoms are great for people who do the ironing. But if you work from home and dress casually, those pieces will end up being donated to charity. So consider your lifestyle, how your usual day looks like, what you do, where you usually go. Write down all areas of your life that need to be taken into consideration when creating your wardrobe. Your clothes should be functional for those purposes.

2. Think about colors

For creating a capsule wardrobe, you need items in colors you can match with all of the others. Black, white, brown, denim, gray, khaki—these are all colors good for basics.

"But will I have to wear only neutrals?!" you ask. No, you don't need to wear neutrals all the time.

That would make anyone bored. You should also have pieces, tops, and T-shirts in colorful prints, as well as items that can be interesting to accessorize and that will make an outfit personal and stylish.

3. Invest in quality over quantity. Give up on fast fashion

You don't need cheap sweaters that you wear only two or three times before they become trash. A full closet doesn't mean you have a lot to wear, remember? Now when you don't buy much anymore, you are free to afford more expensive, quality pieces that will last for many years and that can be enjoyed for a long time.

4. Pajamas don't count!

You need to have this category; let's call it "necessities." This is for all the extra stuff you need—pajamas, underwear, big comfy shirts, workout clothes, scarves, mittens, caps, a swimsuit, and clothes for special weather like a winter jacket and boots.

5. Create modules

Modules are groups of clothes that all mix and match together. You will need a few modules. To create one, choose three tops and two bottoms. Make sure that each top goes with each bottom.

Add one more piece—an outlier, like a jacket or blazer. From those six pieces, you will get 12 outfits.

If you create one more module of pieces you can blend with each other and with the first module, you will have 12 pieces to create 72 outfits. Choose six more pieces to create one more module that you can mix and match with the other two, and you will have 216 options to wear for those 18 pieces. Wow! Could you imagine 216 outfit combinations from your old, overflowing closet? That's one more example that proves less is more.

6. Don't forget your basics

They are the glue that holds your wardrobe together and gives you the versatility you want.

What are the basics?

- a simple dress
- a classic white T-shirt
- a pencil (black) skirt (for a professional look)
- a classic white blouse
- a traditional chambray shirt
- a classic leather jacket
- black dress-pants
- classic blue skinny jeans

- a traditional black blazer
- a denim jacket
- a silk chemise
- a traditional trench coat

7. Incorporate some prints and nice accessories

They can effortlessly change a look completely. Choose boots, a necklace, or earrings that go with each outfit to get some variety without too much effort.

8. Make your own catalog

Take a photo of each outfit and store all those images in one place. It's easy to say that you have 216 possible outfits in your closet, but do you know what they are? This way, you won't have to think about it. Just mix and match the pictures and shine!

Minimalism and Food: Eat What Truly Nourishes You

Practicing a minimalistic approach in all the areas of your life will bring you many benefits. Sooner or later, your minimalistic lifestyle will affect the way you eat. You'll want to be more intentional about what you're putting into your body. If decluttering has so much positive impact on other aspects of your life, think about what a minimalistic approach to food can do for you. In general, your food should be healthy, enjoyable, easy to make, and sustainable.

Don't stockpile your food. A better way is to go to the grocery store more often and buy smaller amounts of food so you always have it fresh and stay within your budget. Going once a week might be a good solution. Find out what works the best for you. You don't need tons of leftovers that get wasted.

Again, quality over quantity. You don't need a lot of meat, but you should be sure that your proteins come from the right source. It would be ideal for it to be grass-fed and organic.

Eat as few processed foods as possible. Raw vegetables, fruits, and high-quality products are a far better choice. Avoid food that is highly processed, stored for a long period of time, transported, and full of additives and preservatives. We aren't saying you have to grow it yourself in your own garden, but try to eat whole foods in their purest form possible.

Minimize the amount of sugar in your diet. Sugar has addictive properties and will only make you hungry for more. It takes a few days to break the habit of eating sugar.

Keep the ingredients for each meal to a minimum. It's simple, quick, and easy. You can prepare many delicious meals and spend just a little time doing it this way.

Last but not least, simple eating will allow you to spend less time in the kitchen for cooking and cleaning up. You can create a habit of using a limited number of dishes, pans, and kitchen utensils, and also wash up while you're cooking. This will leave you with far less work for later.

How to Create a Simple, Minimalist Kitchen You'll Enjoy Cooking in

Since the kitchen is the heart of every home, it's crucial to maintain it clean, tidy, and minimal. Having a minimalist kitchen with only a few knick-knacks will easily allow you to keep it clean and neat. You will enjoy cooking more, have less cleanup work, and spend less time in the kitchen.

Here are some tricks and advice on how to achieve and maintain a sleek, minimal look for your kitchen and spend more time cooking than cleaning.

Keep all of your surfaces clean

Kitchen counters should not be a drop-off place for mail, purses, keys, and other stuff you put down as soon as you walk in. Instead, find a permanent home for those things. The front of the fridge is also a surface, a big one actually. If you usually leave notes to yourself on it, it's time to turn to digital reminders and leave this surface flat and clean.

Remove countertops appliances

If you keep your coffee maker, blender, toaster, stand mixer, or juicer out on your counters, they will be hard to keep clean and make everything look cluttered. Keep only one or two appliances out that you use most frequently. Store the rest in your low cabinets and you'll free up a lot of space.

Don't let the clutter accumulate again

Once you purge your kitchen, never allow clutter to build up again. Check it regularly, once a month for instance, and discard everything you don't need or use.

Use a clear drawer organizer and spice organizer

This will help to keep things ordered and tidy, and you can easily see what's inside.

Develop a habit of cleaning pots and pans immediately

Nothing can make your kitchen look messy as much as dirty dishes. The most practical option is to put a dirty pan or a pot in the sink immediately after finishing cooking and fill it with water. Then you can enjoy your meal and the quick cleanup, too. A clean kitchen will impact your mindset, and you'll be motivated and inspired to keep it tidy and simple all the time.

Invest in high-quality cookware sets that nest inside each other. This will save you a lot of space and provide all the sizes you will ever need. It may be expensive, but you will use them each day for a long, long time. So invest in stainless steel, cast iron, or other durable materials. It's a very cost-effective idea in the long run.

Keep decor simple

Be intentional with your color palette. You can use simple jars for ingredients, cutting boards, cookbooks, fresh herbs, plants, and a bowl of fruit. Remember that a minimalist kitchen shouldn't look sterile and unfriendly, but simple, clean, and tidy.

In case you've been wondering what the minimalist kitchen basics are, here are some suggestions for what you will definitely want to have in your drawers and cabinets:

— two knives—one for chopping vegetables and another for everything else,
— utensils you usually use, like an oversized spoon, a whisk, a steak hammer, a spatula, a ladle, a rolling pin, or whatever you use regularly—one of each is enough,
  - a boiling pot—at least one big one,
  - a frying pan,
  - one set of measuring spoons and measuring cups,
  - a strainer,
  - a grater,
  - a peeler,
  - a glass bowl,

- glass containers for food storage,
- a cutting board,
- a blender,
- plates, mugs, and glasses—one of a kind for each person, plus five for guests.

The Minimalistic Workout: Exercise in a Joyful Way

Getting in shape is one of the best things you can do for yourself. But why do so many of us not feel good about it? It should make us feel good, right? You don't want to be stressed out and overwhelmed by weight loss strategies that don't work. Instead, you need a plan that you'll be able to stick to for a long time.

If traditional approaches, like counting calories and high-intensity exercises, don't work for you, you need to find a better strategy for yourself. This is also where minimalism can help you. The main principle—"get rid of everything that doesn't matter so that you can focus on the important things"—is something that can be applied to your fitness routine as well.

Why do we overcomplicate healthy living?

The fitness industry made it all too complicated so that they could earn more money. They want to convince you that you need to purchase a gym membership, personal trainers, fitness programs and packages, supplements, and gear and gadgets that you don't actually need. But you think you need that stuff to live a healthier lifestyle. And what is more important than health?

Let's take running, for example. What do you need to go running? A pair of comfortable sneakers and a bottle of water. But the industry wants to convince you that you need overpriced running shoes, running shorts and leggings, a top in some neon color, a sports bra, a vitaminized drink, a running belt, a pedometer, GPS tracker, and even more. Instead of spending a ton of money on things you don't need, here are some tips for applying a minimalistic approach to fitness.

Do what you enjoy

If you hate running, don't force yourself to run. Go swimming instead. If you are not into sports, start walking, doing yoga, take dance classes, or do something else. If you think you hate all exercise, you probably just haven't found the right type of exercise for you. Once you find what works for you, enjoy it and have fun—you'll be more likely to stick with it.

Don't go on a diet—change your lifestyle for good

Diets simply don't work. You may see the results from dieting, but in the long-term, it's not a solution. They are hard to stick to and then it's difficult to maintain the results. It can be overwhelming, especially if you count calories or your diet has a bunch of specific rules. It demands a lot of attention and energy, it's not healthy, and it's not enjoyable at all.

But changing habits is a long-term game changer. Try to simplify your diet (as we already discussed). Cut down on sugar and processed foods, and turn to whole fruits and veggies. The results will be obvious, long-lasting, and you won't be stressed out about food, but full of energy for more important things.

Focus on health

If you focus only on appearance, you will never be completely satisfied. There will always be something to work on. But if you focus on health and measure your success according to your energy, vitality, mobility, and strength, you will see how far you have come. You will always be motivated yet satisfied and will be able to appreciate the possibilities of your body.

Use less of everything—exercise, time, equipment

Focus on the most impactful exercises for big muscles and forget everything else. Do some warm-ups and stretches, then squats, deadlifts, bench presses, pull-ups, and core work. Pack it all in about 20 minutes per day and it's enough.

You don't need expensive equipment. A simple mat and your body weight are usually enough. If you go to a gym, stick to good old barbells, kettlebells, and dumbbells.

Keep your exercise sessions short and intense. The main point is to save more time for more important things while getting results.

Start easy

If you are new to working out, give yourself time to adapt to a new routine. Do your best to learn the correct technique and go easy on yourself.

Be consistent

If your routine is simple, it's harder to give up or skip it. During stressful times, it's better to do what you can instead of abandoning your routine or give it up. When tasks are complicated, it's easier to procrastinate or give up. Make it simple and stick to the routine on a constant basis.

Progress gradually

It's better than pushing yourself the first week, burning out, and then recovering. Slow progress is stable and durable.

Focus on essentials

This means mobility, strength, and cardio. If you work smarter instead of working harder, you will decrease the time spent in the gym and still achieve results.

How to Create a Minimalistic Schedule and Do More of What Makes You Happy

If there is a ton of stuff going on and not enough time for everything, your schedule is cluttered and it's time for a change. As minimalism is all about limiting the non-important things to focus on essentials, your life can't be minimalistic as long as you're constantly running from one activity to another. What you need to make time for is savoring life, enjoying what you love, and what truly matters. You need free space to express yourself, use your talents and knowledge, and create something meaningful.

Accept the fact that you can't do everything

Admit this reality and acknowledge that you have limited resources. You can only do so much. As you can't do it all, you should eliminate clutter. What constitutes clutter in our schedules? All those things that might entertain you, but lead nowhere—at least not to the life you want. For instance, this could be mindless Facebook scrolling or binge-watching series on Netflix. List your priorities and remove the rest.

How to define your priorities?

These are the things most important to you. We all have different priorities and only you can decide on yours. What are your values? What do you want to accomplish? What is your plan? All this will impact your decisions and your life day by day. Think about what you want to be, what kind of person. What are your most significant relationships? What do you want to achieve? List your goals and values and don't lose sight of them.

What's your plan? How will you get there?

Think about what would be the best way to become and do what you want. What actions are required? What should you do in a daily, monthly, even a year-long plan? If you don't want life to toss you like a beach ball from one circumstance to another, you need to decide on your route.

You have to say "No"

If you want to have an option to say "yes" for things you want and love, you need to say "no" to the others.

There will be tough times, some people will be disappointed, but you have to put your priorities first. If someone gets mad, it's their problem, not yours. Most people won't care anyway. You will gain the freedom to spend your time intentionally. Your time on this planet is a limited resource. So say "no" to coffee with not-so dear friend in order to be able to enjoy more time with your kids, for example.

Do one thing at a time. Put an end to multitasking. You will probably finish a similar amount of tasks, but without the stress. Slowly and consciously finish one, and then go on to the next task on your to-do list. No rush—you are not in a hurry. You are enjoying your life, remember?

Find what motivates and inspires you and do it

We are not here to be slaves. In order to enjoy and celebrate this life, do as much as you can of what you love. That's what minimalism all about—discarding other things from your schedule to make time for being present, conscious, and aware of life so you can enjoy it.

How to Be a Minimalist and Raise Happy Kids

While researching minimalism, you might see many single people or people without kids, who live with only the basics. They pack their backpack and go travel the world. That's nice, you think, but not for me. With two or three kids, it's simply not possible.

Being minimalist with kids is indeed far more difficult, but it's also more important than ever. By living a minimalist lifestyle, we teach our kids a lot of crucial things about life. They learn it's not all about material stuff. They learn to be generous, to share, to think in an eco-friendly way. They learn about boundaries and we, as a family, spend much more time together in fun activities and making memories. We are closer and calmer. They will grow up in a peaceful environment with calm parents who are fully present and focused on what really matters. Children may not listen to you, but they are watching you all the time. They learn by following your example.

Here is some guidance on how to become or stay a minimalist (even) with little ones.

You first

Don't begin the decluttering process with your kid's stuff. Just don't. It's not fair and looks like a punishment. Declutter your belongings first—your clothes, your kitchen, garage, papers, drawers, shelves, everything. Then you can turn to the kids' rooms. They will see your example and want to engage.

Explain why and include them

It's always a good idea to explain to kids why they should do what they should. So talk to them about all the benefits you as a family will gain from having less stuff. Use the language according to their age so they can understand you. Be enthusiastic about minimalism (but not too much or you could put yourself at risk of not being trusted).

Once you have explained how wonderful your life can be without too much stuff, include kids in the process. Let them decide what to keep and actively engage them in decluttering, reorganizing, and decorating their rooms.

When you are letting your kids decide what to keep and what to discard, look for physical boundaries or limitations. It's more convenient for them to clearly see how much they can keep. For instance, they can keep as many toys as can be put into a closet. Or they can keep as much as can fit on a shelf or in a box. If they want to keep something it's ok, but if there's no more space in the box, they have to decide what to toss away in order to free up some space. So if your kids tend to be little hoarders, let them keep whatever they want as long as it can be put into a drawer, for example.

Boundaries are important for kids to feel safe. Saying no to them is extremely significant if you want them to grow into adults who protect their own and respect those of others.

Clothes

To stay minimal with kids and not make your house cluttered again, consider creating a capsule wardrobe for everyone. Mom, dad, and kids (as many of them as you have) can have a beautiful mix-and-match wardrobe. This will make it easier for everyone to dress themselves and also to look well put-together.

It's also wise to store kids' clothing in a way that they can reach it, dress themselves, and put it back in its place.

Also, everyone in a family should have one memory box. It's the safest place for keepsakes and stuff with sentimental value, and it will also ensure that there isn't too much of it.

When it comes to shopping...

Keep yourself from buying things your kids might need in the future. Purchase only stuff they need now—clothes in their current size, toys they will play with at the right age, books they can understand now, and so on. You can't anticipate what they will need or want in the future. Make their present as joyful as you can.

Paper clutter with kids

Once they start going to preschool, paper clutter will fill your house. They will bring several projects home from school every day. You can choose to keep what's important, something they managed to make for the first time. You can keep the paper where your child managed to write their name for the first time. Later, you can let them decide what is truly important. For now, keep what's meaningful to you. Discard the rest without feeling guilty, otherwise you'll end up living in a nest of paper clutter.

Simplify their food

More often than not, children like simple foods. For instance, boiled vegetables with nothing on them. Give them what they want. It cuts down on waste and also the waste of your nerves and spent energy. Of course you should feed them healthy meals, but try to find balance instead of insisting on what they don't want to eat.

Toys

When it's about the majority of kids' stuff, their toys, hold to one simple rule—all toys live in their room or a playroom. How many toys does a kid actually need?

According to an extremely minimalist approach, children don't need toys at all. They have enough imagination and can find everything they need for play in nature. If this sounds too extreme for you, you're not alone. Kids are good for kids' own development, that's for sure.

We have already talked about which kinds of toys to keep while decluttering, but here's a short list of recommended toys (we talk about kinds of toys, not particular items; you probably already have something from each category):

- building blocks
- a doll or a teddy bear
- characters—little people, animals
- a ball
- art supplies
- scarves that can be used as costumes
- a swing or a mat

- vehicles
- books
- sensory boxes with beans, rice, pasta, water, sand.

Simplifying and going minimal with kids is beneficial for the whole family. Less time in cleaning and tidying means more quality time with your kids and creating memories.

Don't Be a Snail: How to Travel like a Minimalist

It's obvious how minimalism principles can serve you if you want to travel the world. You want to collect experiences, chase adventures, meet new people, and learn about different civilizations and a variety of customs and cultures, not to carry around heavy luggage. Everything you might need can be put in one well-packed backpack.

As for everything else, we want to be intentional about what we take with us. For each item you want to pack, ask yourself a few questions: What's the worst situation I could find myself in if I didn't have this item? Don't skip this question. Too often, people carry a ton of stuff "just in case" for every possible situation that often never happens.

Also ask yourself: Do I love this item? Is it lightweight? Is it multifunctional?

Then, some general advice would be to use packing cubes, because they make packing simpler. Also, the best way to pack your clothes is to roll each item to take up less space.

Here's a list of the most basic stuff you should pack for traveling, regardless of whether you're going on a ten-day vacation or a five-year trip around the world:

- passport
- international driver's license, if you have one
- wallet with cash and cards
- travel insurance
- laptop or MacBook
- iPhone
- camera
- power bank
- external hard disc
- 5x T-shirts
- 2x pants
- 2x shorts
- 1x jacket
- 1x swimsuit or swim shorts
- 1x scarf
- 1x cap
- 6x socks
- 6x underwear
- 2x bra
- 1x flip-flops
- 1x shoes
- a daily journal
- a cable bag
- a cosmetic bag
- a nice quality backpack

The Art of Less: Slowing Down and Simplifying

If having more and more stuff was the way to happiness, there would be many more happy people. Yet there are even millionaires who are depressed. Maybe it's time for us to start searching elsewhere. What if going in the opposite direction, getting rid of material belongings, could bring us the peace, joy, and fulfillment we seek?

Minimalism is not about wiping down your floors or having all your socks organized by color. It's not even about always having tidy house. It's a unique mindset, a particular philosophy you can apply to all areas of your life.

Once you begin thinking like a minimalist, you will be more intentional about whatever you are doing. You'll always tend to eliminate distractions and excessive details so you can be more present, more deliberate, and focus on what truly matters. You'll never again be in a position where you can't see the wood for the trees. You'll want to make your house a home, a sanctuary for you and your family to recharge and enjoy being together.

You won't worry about meaningless things. You'll direct your energy in some other more constructive way. You'll finally do what you love and have enough space, time, and energy to enjoy the life you have always known that you deserve. You won't live in a house full of the past. Instead, you will enjoy the present and welcome the future with open arms.

Now when you finally have some extra time and extra money (because you no longer shop out of habit), you can do a lot of things. Here are some ideas for you:

- Read a book.
- Drink tea or coffee in silence.
- Listen to music.
- Meditate.
- Go for a walk.
- Play with your kids.
- Play with a pet.
- Cuddle with your spouse.
- Bake a cake.
- Grow your garden.
- Do yoga.
- Go out with friends.
- Paint.
- Draw.
- Write.
- Dance.
- Plan a trip.
- Do your nails.

- Take a warm, bubble bath.
- Do whatever makes you happy.

In closing, one more thing to be aware of is that although minimalism might be the right mindset for you, it doesn't have to work for everyone else. Many people have managed to achieve balance practicing minimalism, including my clients and myself. But it's not the only way to achieve serenity and well-being. Be flexible, empathetic, and full of understanding for everyone and everything. Live your life the way that's best for you, and let others do the same for themselves. If you have to choose between being happy or being right, always choose the first solution. Because being happy is the crucial, ultimate goal for everyone and you, as a minimalist, focus only on the essentials.

Printed in Great Britain
by Amazon